D0603489

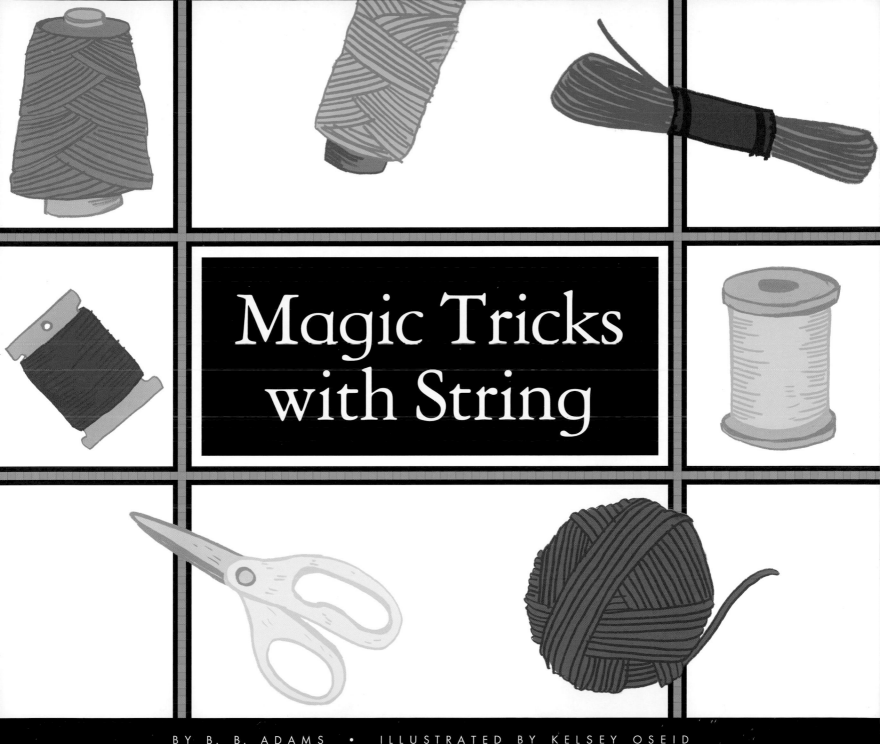

Magic Tricks
with String

BY B. B. ADAMS • ILLUSTRATED BY KELSEY OSEID

The Child's World

Published by The Child's World®
1980 Lookout Drive • Mankato, MN 56003-1705
800-599-READ • www.childsworld.com

Acknowledgments
The Child's World®: Mary Berendes, Publishing Director
Red Line Editorial: Editorial direction and production
The Design Lab: Design

Photographs ©: iStockphoto/Thinkstock, 4

ISBN: 978-1623235611
LCCN: 2013931435

Printed in the United States of America
Mankato, MN
July, 2013
PA02176

ABOUT THE AUTHOR

B. B. Adams writes trivia, humor, and fiction in books and on the Internet. He lives in Oregon with his family.

ABOUT THE ILLUSTRATOR

Kelsey Oseid is an illustrator and graphic designer from Minneapolis, Minnesota. When she's not drawing, she likes to do craft projects, bake cookies, go on walks, and play with her two cats, Jamie and Fiona. You can find her work at www.kelseyoseid.com.

Table of Contents

Simple as String!

Have you ever watched a **magician** put on a magic show? Magic may seem hard. But it can be super simple. Can you tie a knot? Then you can do magic!

In this book you will find six fun magic tricks. All you will need is string and not much else. Ask a parent to help you find string that will work well for these tricks. Have fun. Try your best. Now let's make some magic!

PUT ON A SHOW!
Becoming a magician takes a lot of practice. Practice your tricks in a mirror. Have an adult help you learn them. Then you can show them to an **audience**. You could even wear a magician's hat or a cape!

For the tricks in this book, you'll need:

- String
- 2 identical rings
- Printer paper
- Scissors
- Coin
- Scarf
- Straight drinking straw

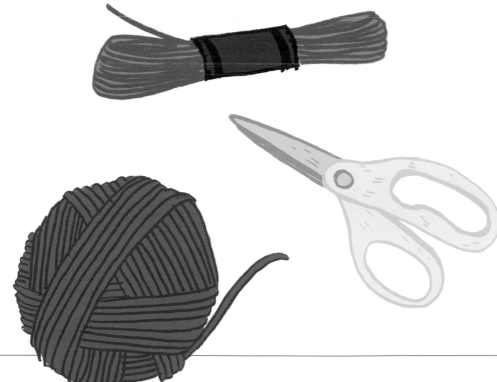

SAFETY TIPS
Some of the tricks in this book use scissors. Scissors can be sharp! Never run with scissors. Don't wave them at others. Make sure to use safety scissors. And always keep your fingers out of the way. They are a magician's most important tools!

WHAT YOU'LL NEED:
- One 24-inch-long (61 cm) piece of string

Magical Knot

Wow your audience when you magically tie a string without ever letting go of the ends!

STEP 2

1 Start out by asking for a volunteer from the audience. Tell her to hold each end of the string in her hands. Ask her to tie a knot in the string without letting go of the ends. She won't be able to!

2 Now it's your turn. First cross your arms. Your

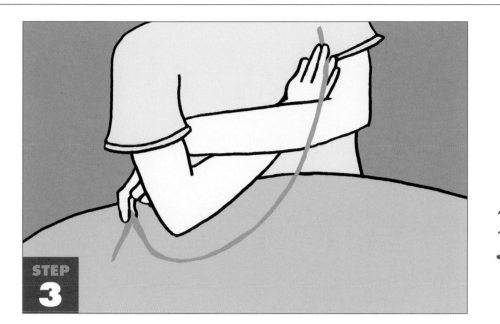

left hand should be tucked behind your right elbow. Your right hand should be in front of your left elbow.

3 Now bend over. Pick up the ends of the string with each hand. Keep your arms crossed!

4 Now just uncross your arms. The ends of the string will move with your hands. The string will be tied in a knot.

You tied a knot without letting go of the string!

String and Paper Cut

You'll amaze your audience with this next trick.

1 Start by folding section **A** of the paper down. Fold up section **C** so it overlaps with section **A**.

2 Trick time! Tuck the string into the crease between section **C** and **B**.

3 Now fold **A** down over **B**. Then fold **C** down

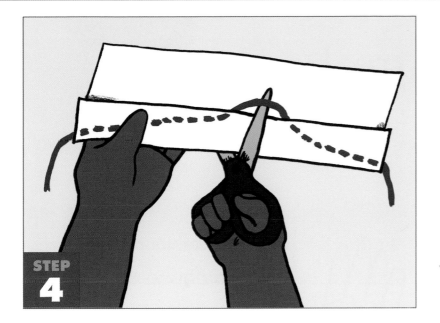

over **A**. Use your thumb to catch a loop of string outside of the fold. The ends of the string should hang out of the paper. Make sure the fold faces you.

4 Next take your scissors. Cut through the paper near the middle. Slide your scissors under the loop of string.

5 Now crumple up the two halves of paper. Then pull out the uncut string.

Your audience won't believe their eyes!

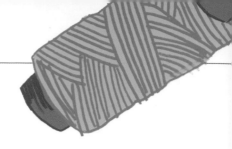

All Thumbs

WHAT YOU'LL NEED:
- One 12-inch (30 cm) piece of string (a slippery string works best)

In this trick, you will use magic to undo the knots tying your thumbs together.

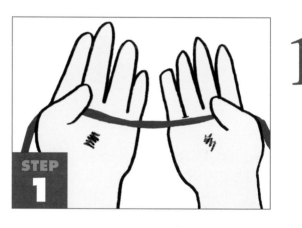

1 Hold your hands with **palms** facing up. Ask a friend to lay the string across your hands. The string should be tucked between your thumbs and your palms.

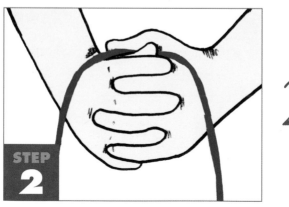

2 Keep holding the string. Fold your hands across each other. Knit your fingers together.

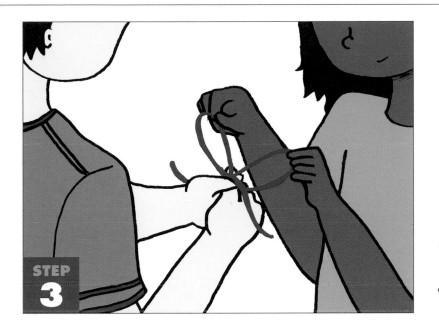

Tuck your left ring finger under your right middle finger. Stack your thumbs. Your left thumb should be on top of your right thumb.

3 Ask your friend to tie the string around your thumbs. She should use a loose bow. Tuck your hidden ring finger into the loop inside your folded hands.

4 Now tell her you can magically escape. Use your hidden ring finger to pull the string on the inside.

The loop will come undone. Your thumbs will come untied!

WHAT YOU'LL NEED:
- One 36-inch (91 cm) piece of string
- 1 straight drinking straw
- Scissors

The Cut and Uncut String

In this trick you will cut a piece of string. Then you will magically put it back together!

STEP 1

1 Before you do the trick, carefully cut a small opening in the middle of one side of your straw. The opening should be about 3 inches (7 cm) long. Make sure your audience never sees the opening.

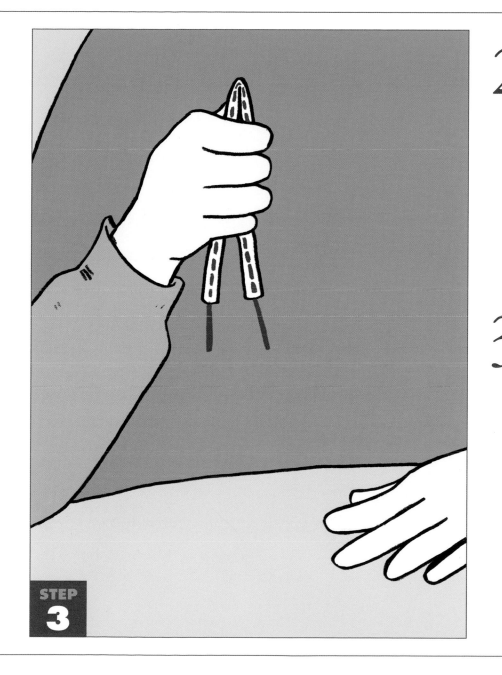

2 Now bring in the audience. Thread the string through the straw. The ends of the string should hang out each side. Make sure to hold the straw so the opening you cut faces you.

3 Next fold the straw in half down the middle. Make a fist around the folded straw so just the top peeks out.

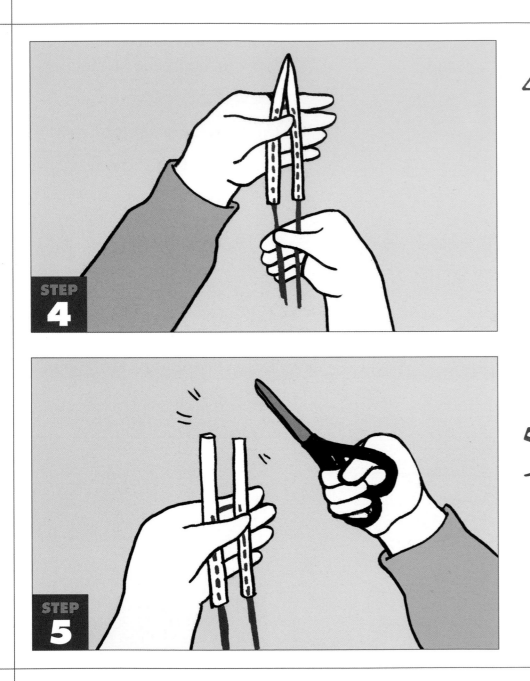

4 Pull the ends of your string tightly. This will cause the middle of the string to pop out of the opening. Now you can release your fist. But make sure you hide the string popping out of the opening. Use your finger to cover it.

5 Now just cut the top of the folded straw. Pull the ends apart. This proves you have really cut the straw.

6 Next put the two ends back together. Make a loose fist around the two ends. Say a magic word like *abracadabra*!

7 Then just pull the uncut string out from the straw.

You have magically put the string back together!

STEP
7

Finger-Palm Position

The last trick uses one of the most important tricks in a magician's toolbox. It will help you do many more magic tricks. The finger-palm trick allows you to hide small things in your hand. Practice the following steps with a coin. Soon you'll have the hang of it.

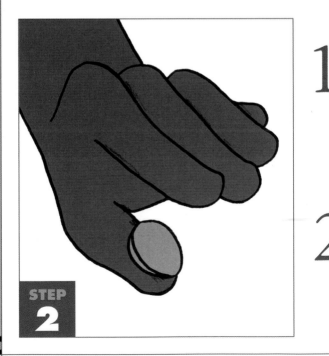

STEP
2

1 Start out by holding the coin between your thumb and your pointer finger.

2 Now stretch out your other fingers. Raise your pointer finger to join the rest of your

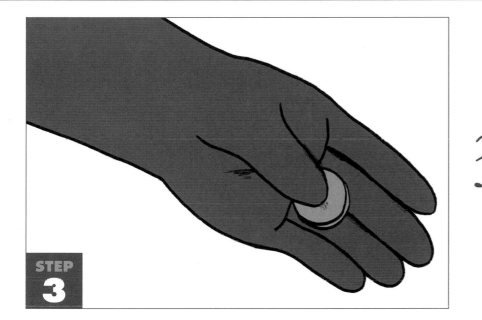

STEP 3

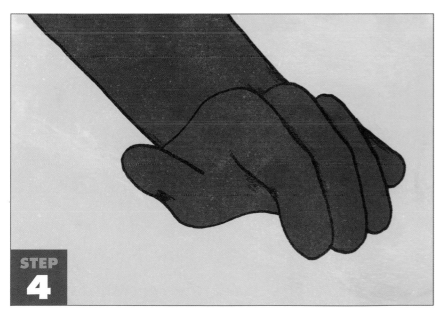

STEP 4

hand. The coin should balance on your thumb.

3 Next carefully lift your thumb. Tuck the coin into the bottom of your fingers. The coin should be between the end of your palm and your first **knuckles**.

4 Now release your thumb. The coin should be snug in your fingers. Practice holding the coin. Your hand should look natural.

Practice this movement over and over. Soon your audience won't see you hide the coin.

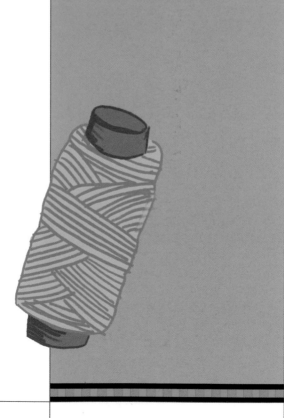

- One 36-inch (91 cm) piece of string
- 2 identical rings, (small key rings work well)
- 1 light scarf
- 2 friends

The Ring Release

This next trick is a little bit harder. Ask an adult to help you learn the trick. The secret to being a good magician is practice! Follow the steps below to learn how to magically remove a ring from a piece of string.

STEP
2

1 Before doing the trick, hide **ring 1** in your hand using the **Finger-Palm Position**. Put **ring 2** on a table so your friends can see it.

2 Now bring in your audience. Start by

asking each of your friends to hold an end of the string.

3 Ask one friend to pick up **ring** 2 from the table and put it on the string. Have him slide it to the middle.

4 Put the scarf on top of the string. It should cover **ring** 2.

5 Tell your friends to pull each end of string. They should leave a little bit of **slack** in the middle. Now put both of your hands under the scarf.

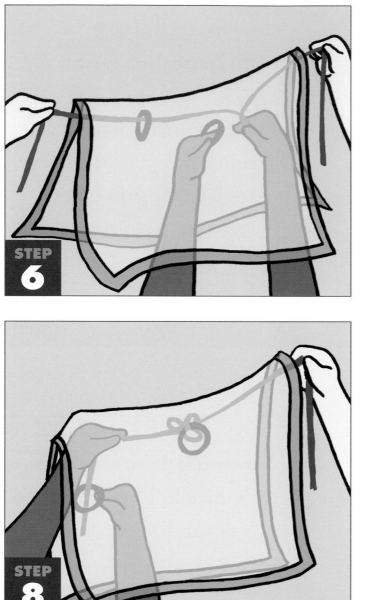

6 You have been holding **ring 1** this entire time. Now take the slack on the string. Push a small loop of string through the center of **ring 1**. Use the loop to loosely tie the ring to the string.

7 Ask one of your friends to gently shake the string. Tell him he isn't doing it right. Walk over to show him how. Drag the threaded **ring 2** with you as you walk.

8 Take the end of the string from your friend. Secretly slide **ring 2** off the string.

9 **Finger palm** the ring.

STEP 11

FOOL YOUR FANS
Magicians fool people by making the audience look at one thing. Then the magician can do something else. This is called **misdirection**. Showing your friend how to swing the string is an example of this. It gives you the chance to pull off the ring while your friend is **distracted**.

10 Now hand the string back to your friend. Place your hand on the scarf over **ring** 1. Pull off the scarf with the hand holding **ring** 2.

11 Untie the loose knot and let the ring fall to the floor. The ring is free!

Your audience will be amazed!

Glossary

audience (AW-dee-uhns): An audience is the group of people that watches your tricks. Practice your tricks before showing them to an audience.

distracted (di-STRAKT-id): People are distracted when their attention is called away from something. Try secret magic moves while your audience is distracted.

knuckles (NUHK-uhlz): Knuckles are the joints in a person's finger. To hold an object in the finger palm position, you should tuck it between your palm and your first knuckles.

magician (muh-JISH-uhn): A magician is a person who performs magic tricks. True magicians never reveal their secrets.

misdirection (mis-duh-REK-shuhn): Misdirection means to call someone's attention away from something by causing them to focus on something else. Asking your friend to focus on swaying the string is a misdirection.

palms (PAHMZ): Your palms are the flat, inside parts of your hands. You can hide things in your palms using the finger-palm trick.

slack (SLAK): Slack is the part of a rope or string that is not tight. You can use the slack in the string to tie on a ring.

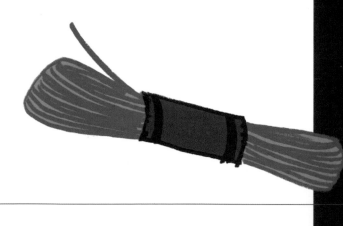

Learn More

Books

Gordon, Lynn. *52 Cool Tricks for Kids*. San Francisco, CA: Chronicle Books, 2008.

Ho, Oliver. *Young Magician: Magic Tricks*. New York: Sterling, 2003.

Web Sites

Visit our Web site for links about magic tricks with string: *childsworld.com/links*

Note to Parents, Teachers, and Librarians: We routinely verify our Web links to make sure they are safe and active sites. So encourage your readers to check them out!

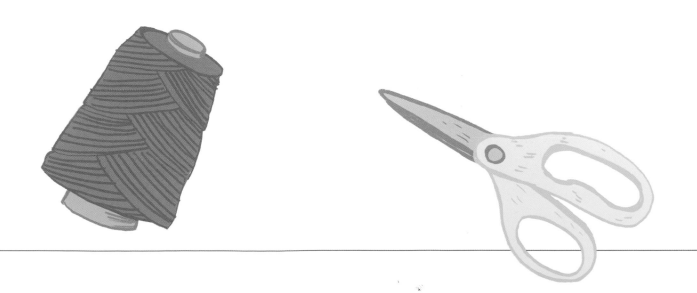

Index

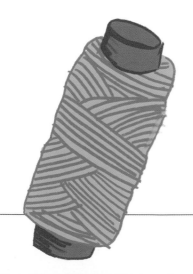